Let's READ!

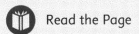

🔖 Read the Page

⭐ Game

🔷 🔷 🔷
Say It Sound It Spell It

🔄 Repeat

⬛ Stop

ABC Snack Time

Mm Nn Oo Pp Qq

Rr Ss Tt Uu Vv

Ww Xx Yy Zz

1

The Vowel

a

e

hat

bib

wig

bat

rat

lips

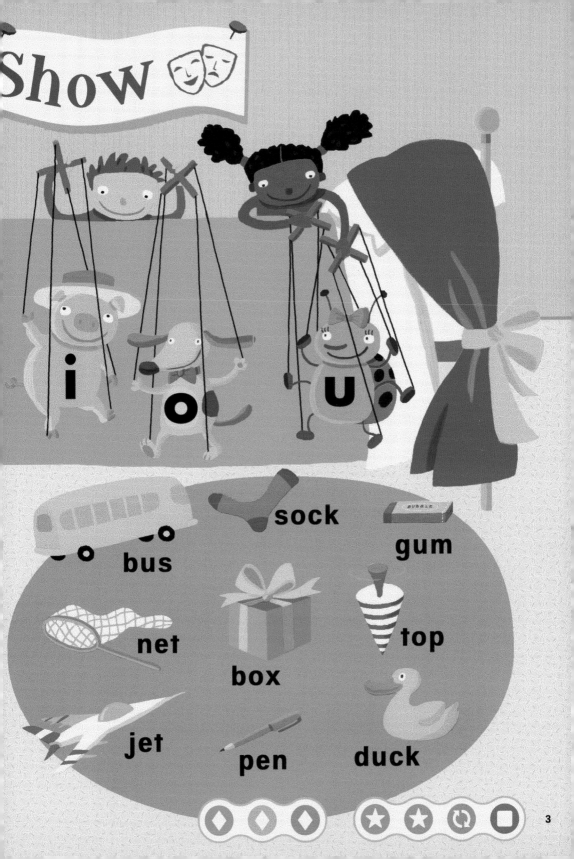

Show

i   o   u

bus   sock   gum

net   box   top

jet   pen   duck

3

pen

hen

WORD

pig

wig

hat

cat

fox

box

bug

rug

4

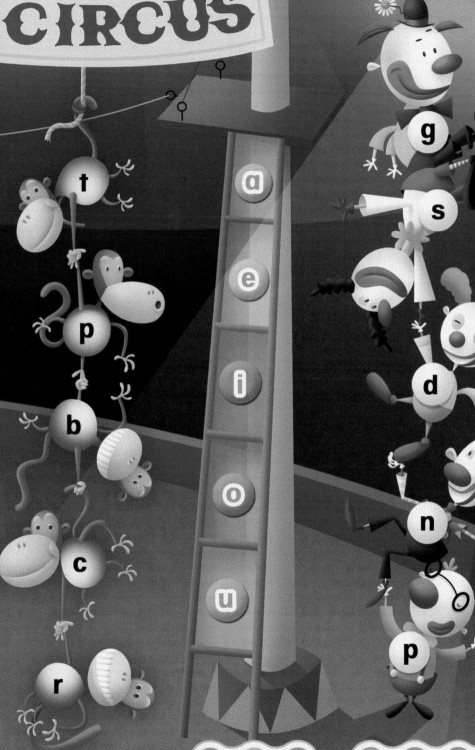

CIRCUS

t
p
b
c
r

a
e
i
o
u

g
s
d
n
p

5

The Special Lunch

 Leap made himself a .

"What a great big lunch," said.

He spread chocolate sauce and

on some fresh-baked raisin .

He added a

underneath some jam,

3 slices of some , and

1 slice of yummy .

Leap ran down to the

to show his  the treat.

But when he opened up his

his lunch fell on his !

Leap's started rumbling.

He was hungry as a !

"Don't worry, Leap," said ,

"you can share my , of course."

Pattern Place

Skip Counting

1   2   3   4   5

11   12   13   14   15

21   22   23   24   25

31   32   33   34   35

41   42   43   44   45

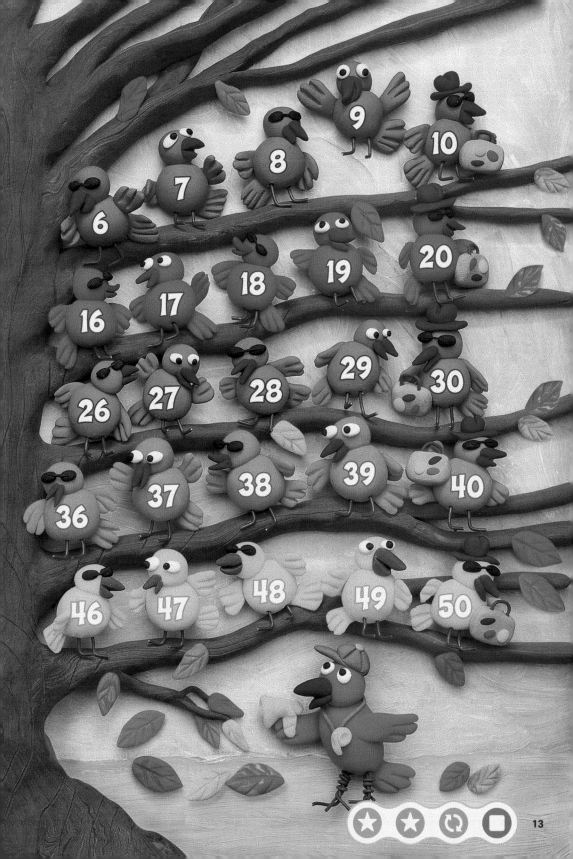

Monster Mathematics

2

3

6

9

5

7

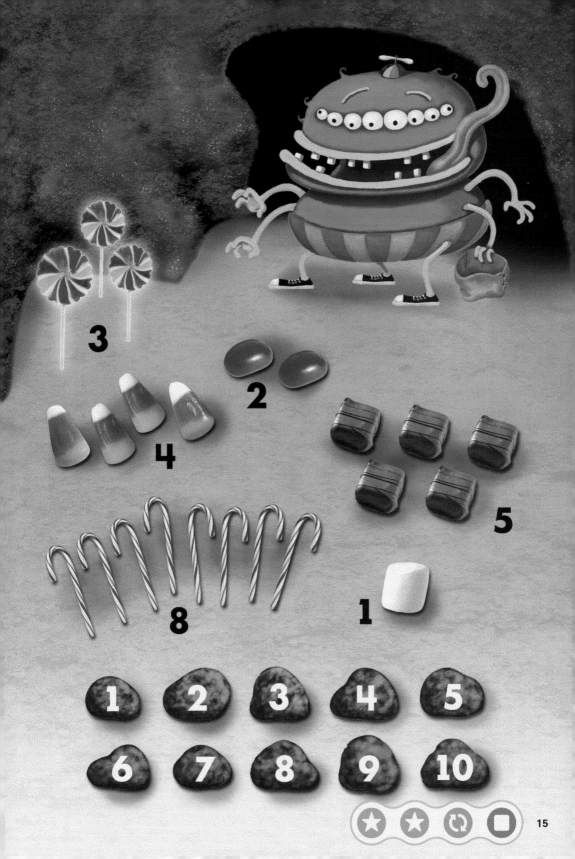

MONTHS AND SEASONS

⭐ January

February

March

April

May

June

July

August

September

October

November

December

WINTER

SPRING

AUTUMN

SUMMER

Party Month!

Sunday	Monday	Tuesday
1	2	3
8	9	10
15	16	17
22	23	24
29	30	31

Wednesday	Thursday	Friday	Saturday
4	5	6	7
11	12	13	14
18	19	20	21
25	26	27	28

My Community

Supermarket

Ice Cream Shop

Park

Radio Station

Police Station

Zoo

Library

School

Hospital

Barber Shop

FIRE STATION

Fire Station

Cinema

POST OFFICE

Post Office

21

Dinosaur Class Photo

Stegosaurus

Brachiosaurus

Velociraptors

Triceratops

Chunk it   Dinner time   Facts

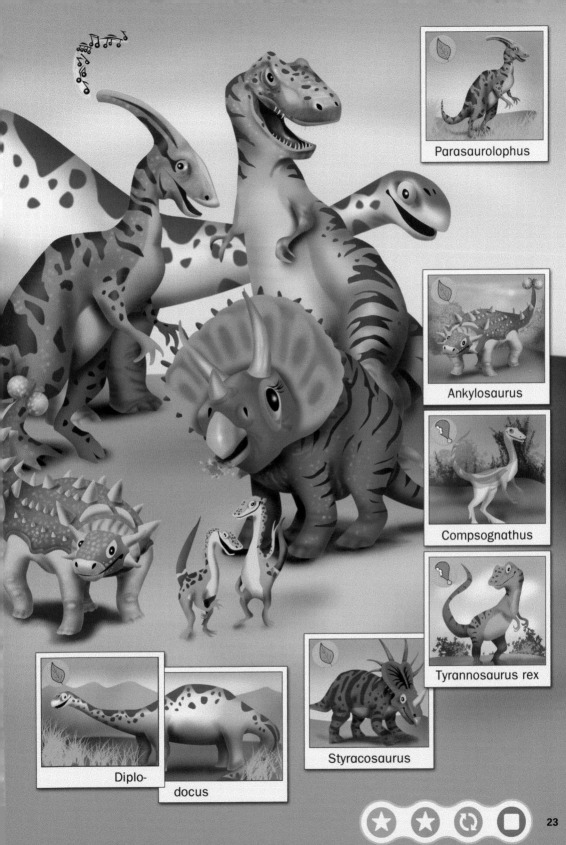

Parasaurolophus

Ankylosaurus

Compsognathus

Tyrannosaurus rex

Diplo-

docus

Styracosaurus

Feelings

sad

silly

scared

angry

happy

silly

sad

25